DUNAMIS

Living the Resurrected Life

Inner Healing Workbook - Series 1

TIM SOWERS
KEISHA SOWERS

Copyright © 2019 The Sowers Ministries

All rights reserved. No part of this publication may be reproduced, stored in a retrieval system, or transmitted in any form or by any means - for example, electronic, photocopy, recording - without the prior written permission of the authors. The only exception is brief quotations in printed reviews.

ISBN:978-0-578-58523-9

Interior Design by Machu
Book Cover Design by Machu
Edited by Uzo Nwiyi

"Cellular Cleansing Prayer" © 2018
Used by permission and contributed by Vaterio Hunter
Voice of Many Waters International AACML

Comfort Circle diagram used by permission

Scripture is taken from BibleGateway.com
The Disciple's Study Bible, New International Version ®, NIV®
Copyright © 1988 by Holman Bible Publishers
All rights reserved.
International Copyright secured.

Contents

HEART CHECK 06

THE COMFORT CIRCLE 12

THE VAULT 16

WHERE IS YESHUA? 19

FASTING 24

TRUTH MEDITATION 28

SOAKING 31

APPENDIX 33

    A. Cellular Cleansing Prayer 34

    B. A Dialogue With God While Reading Ephesians 35

    C. Heart Check Worksheet 37

    D. Truth Meditation Chart 42

    E. Soaking Journal 47

    Books And Resources 52

    About The Authors 53

What is Dunamis?

I had the most impactful revelation about the resurrection power of Yeshua back in 2016.

I met a woman named Deraha in a soaking group in Richmond, Virginia.

She had a heart monitor attached to her, but by the words that came out of her mouth, you would have thought she was the healthiest, most vibrant person in the room.

Since 2017, Deraha has died and come back to life on the operating table over fifteen times. She has held steadfast to her faith in the resurrection power of Jesus through it all.

She used that time to minister to the doctors and nurses in the hospital. While bedridden, she even had the audacity to call us to ask how WE were doing.

She has never magnified the issues she has been through, rather, her mouth speaks of God's goodness and His faithfulness to complete what He has started in her.

She knows that when it is her time to be with Jesus, she will say with peace, "It is finished," just as He did while on the cross.

Deraha knows that the same power, called "*dunamis*" in Greek language, is the same power that resides in her. And upon completion of the *Dunamis* workbook, Deraha is back home, alive, and sassy as ever.

Thank you, Deraha, for representing the dunamis power of Jesus.

May your testimony empower thousands to intimately know Him and His resurrecting power.

How To Use This Workbook

We have written this interactive workbook to support you in the healing process. We are praying that you finish this journey strong and full of peace. We are also praying that you will help others heal through the dunamis power of Yeshua so this will cause a ripple effect across the world.

This workbook is not completely self-guided, but rather a supplement and reference for our sessions and workshops. Inner healing is best conducted within a safe community. We recommend that you schedule a phone, Skype, or in-person session with us for best results.

Keep your heart with all vigilance, for from it flows the springs of life.
Proverbs 4:23

1 Heart Check

What are the top 5 emotions in your heart?

Knowing what is going on inside of our heart at any given moment is a basic step to emotional wellness.

Our emotions can quickly change based off of what someone says, our circumstances, or what we ate for lunch. This unstable state can cause thoughts to enter our mind that can potentially sway us off course and eventually cause disease and physical dysfunction.

Does God want us to have a sound mind and a prosperous soul?

Yes!

So let's aim for the Mind of Christ in all situations, in all things.

Let's aim for His Truth.

Let's aim for peace that passes all understanding.

We have been given dominion over our soul through Christ.

The soul is made up of the mind, will, and emotions.

Our heart can capture both positive and negative emotions.

It is important to be aware of what is going on in our heart because, as the Bible says, "Out of the heart, the mouth speaks." Our words are powerful and can bring forth what we say.

If our heart is full of pain or heaviness, it is because we are meditating on toxic thoughts and the mouth will eventually speak what we are thinking.

Doing heart checks will help take dominion over our mental health and ultimately, our reality.

Heart Check: Step 1

Now, let's find a quiet place.

We are going to identify if we have a heart wall and determine if there are toxic emotions trapped behind the wall in our heart.

1. Ask Your Heart: "Do I Have A Wall Up?"

You must take down the wall first in order to move forward with releasing the trapped negative emotions.

2. Once You Take The Wall Down, Identify The Top 5 Emotions In Your Heart.

Write these down here.

Emotion 1 _____

Emotion 2 _____

Emotion 3 _____

Emotion 4 _____

Emotion 5 _____

3. Beginning With The First Emotion, Identify If The Emotion Is Yours ... Or Is The Emotion Generational?

Emotion 1 _____ Mine/Generational

Emotion 2 _____ Mine/Generational

Emotion 3 _____ Mine/Generational

Emotion 4 _____ Mine/Generational

Emotion 5 _____ Mine/Generational

4. Now, let's take this one emotion at a time. Starting with the first emotion, if it's yours, pray and ask God to help you release it. Sometimes our emotions are easily released, and every now and then, they are stuffed down so deep inside of us (see the Vault), that we may not be ready to release them or need assistance to do so.

   If you are able to release the emotion, write down the process that God gave you to release it. Was it meditating on truth through scripture? Did He take you back to the scene where it happened and show you where Jesus was during the circumstance? There are many ways we can release toxic emotions. Write down your experience with the first emotion here.

   Emotion 1 _____

   _____

   _____

   _____

   _____

   _____

   _____

   _____

   _____

   _____

   _____

   _____

   _____

   _____

   _____

   _____

5. Repeat steps 2-4 for the remaining toxic emotions. Write down how God released you from the emotions below.

   Emotion 2 _____

   _____

   _____

   _____

   _____

Emotion 3

Emotion 4 _____

Emotion 5 _____

Generational Emotions

If any of your emotions are generational, there are a few extra steps you will need to take to release it.

Steps To Release Generational Emotions:

1. Stand in the gap and ask for forgiveness for the generational sins committed.

2. Forgive those who committed the sins.

3. Confess and repent of following along in these sins.

4. Place the cross of Christ between you in your mother's womb and the generational sins.

5. Declare the generational sins to STOP at the cross and no longer affect you or any of your descendants. See the negative sin energy hit the cross until it stops.

6. Ask for the generational blessings that have been hindered due to the sins.

7. Pray a cleansing prayer over you and those that may be present.

8. Give thanks and praise to the Lord.

As you do this important work with Yeshua, the dunamis power inside of you will stop generational curses and release generational blessings. He is setting yourself AND your family line free! How empowering to know that when we heal, we also affect the healing of our family in the process.

More heart check worksheets are located in Appendix C of this workbook as needed.

Even though I walk through the darkest valley, I will fear no evil, for you are with me; your rod and your staff, they comfort me.
Psalm 23:4

2 The Comfort Circle

As a child ... were you listened to by your parents?

In 2014, *Highlights* magazine conducted a national survey, polling over 1500 children ages 6 to 12. In this survey, the majority (62%) of the children said their parents were distracted when the kids attempted to talk to them. Distractions included cell phones, other siblings, television and internet, and work demands.

In our inner healing work over the years, we've found these results consistent in adults we've asked - almost all have had childhood wounds. Many of those wounds were because they were not listened to or comforted properly through touch when they were young.

In the book *How We Love* by Milan and Kay Yerkovich, the Comfort Circle is introduced as a way to change the way you communicate in relationships.

We often use the Comfort Circle to establish a safe space for trust and dialogue to get to the root of childhood emotional wounds or trauma in our sessions.

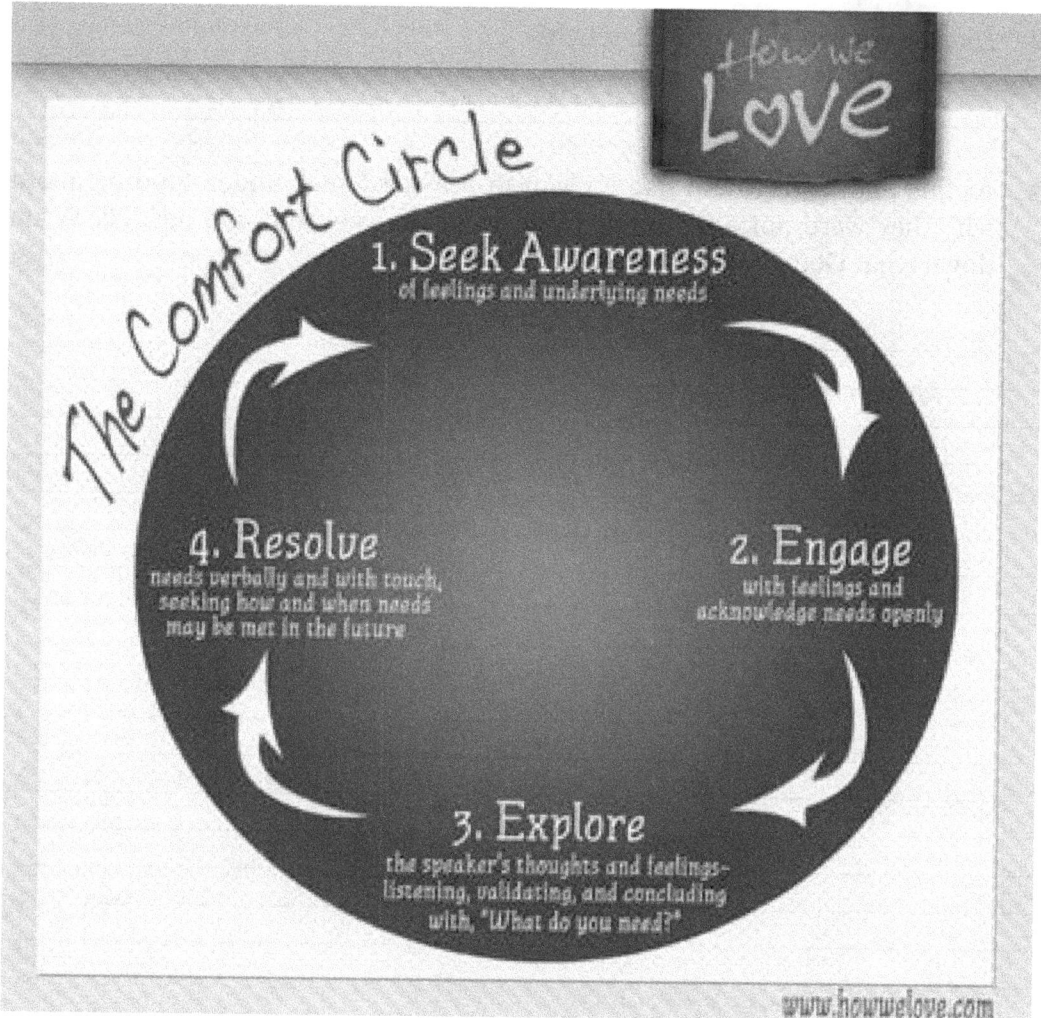

Exercise:

1. Were you listened to by your father when you were young?

   _____

2. Were you comforted by appropriate touch by him as well (hugs, soft pat on the back, etc.)?

   _____

3. How about your mother? Did she usually stop what she was doing to listen to you?

   _____

4. Did she console you through touch?

   _____

5. At this point, we would like for you to pray and seek understanding about why they were not able to comfort you in the way that you needed. Write down what God says to you here.

   _____
   _____
   _____
   _____
   _____
   _____
   _____
   _____
   _____
   _____
   _____
   _____
   _____
   _____
   _____
   _____
   _____
   _____
   _____
   _____

6. Now that you have understanding, can you forgive them and have compassion for them? Why or why not?

   _____
   _____
   _____
   _____
   _____
   _____
   _____

7. Breaking the Cycle (option for parents). If you have children, ask them if you listen to them and console them in the way that they need?. If not, can you make adjustments for them?

Who can discern his errors? Forgive my hidden faults.

Psalm 19:12

3 The Vault

We received revelation about the vault during an inner healing session conducted at a church.

Tim and I were supporting a woman who desired breakthrough but there was an area within her soul that we couldn't access.

In my mind's eye, I saw a spiritual vault in the deepest layer of her soul. It was dark and there were cobwebs around it.

This was when I realized that the Holy Spirit was trying to show me there was something trapped inside of the vault.

There was a padlock on the front as if this woman had unconsciously locked away certain emotions or traumatic experiences for some reason.

When I explained the vision, she started crying uncontrollably. The tears were good - a sign of purging.

I asked her if she was ready to deal with what was inside the vault.

She said yes.

After she prayed and asked God what she had stuffed inside, she shared scenes from her past. We discovered the emotions attached to them. My first inclination was to use one of the healing tools Tim and I were taught from Elijah House and Bethel. However, something unexpected happened.

Holy Spirit said to me, "Ask her what is the combination to the padlock?"

Your Combination

If you sense that you have stuffed emotions and experiences inside, your combination will be unique to your breakthrough.

Like any lock, the combination is different because only you have access to the contents inside.

God will provide freedom for you down to the deepest layers of your soul if you are willing to give Him access.

Some combinations we've discovered:

FAITH, HOPE, and LOVE.
FORGIVENESS, GRACE, and UNDERSTANDING
UNDERSTANDING, FORGIVENESS, and COMPASSION

Not everyone has a vault, but inquire of God to see if you may have some hidden emotions in the deepest layers of your soul.

1. Do you have stuffed emotions inside? If so, please list what God reveals to you here.

_____
_____
_____
_____
_____
_____
_____
_____

2. Is there a particular experience attached to these emotions? If so, please write here.

_____
_____
_____
_____
_____
_____
_____
_____

3. If you are ready to deal with these emotions, ask God what is the combination to heal and then release these areas to Him. Write down the combination and if there is anything else He reveals to you about maintaining freedom in these areas.

The Lord himself goes before you and will be with you; he will never leave you nor forsake you.
Deuteronomy 31:8

4 Where is Yeshua?

One of the greatest assaults from the enemy is to have us think that we are alone in this world.

Afraid or discouraged, we reinforce this lie by thinking back to our childhood or a traumatic event in our life and we replay it over and over.

We even know in the Word that it says hope deferred makes the heart sick.

We can defeat this lie by bringing Jesus into scenes of our lives where we felt abandoned.

Often, during heart checks, a particular emotion is tied into a person's past. We ask for details of what happened and people often cry as they tell the story.

Once they are done, we ask them where was Jesus when this happened.

When they go back into the scene to find Jesus, He has been described as hugging them. Sometimes He will say something to them that brings comfort. Other times He is shielding their body and taking most of the pain for them.

Coffee Chat With Tim

Question: Can you share an emotion that came up during a heart check?

Tim: I was working on rejection. I asked the Holy Spirit to take me to a place where I was first rejected. I saw myself in our living room in Radford, Virginia when I was probably about 4 or 5. I remember watching my mother rocking my younger brother in the chair. I was wondering why I didn't get rocked or get the hugs or attention that he got back then.

Jesus told me that in my mother's time, when kids got to be a certain age, older kids didn't receive hugs so she didn't think I needed to be hugged anymore. They viewed me as jolly all the time, but my heart still desired to get hugs, to have the physical attention, for her to sit and hold me.

Question: Do you feel like you have wholeness in that area? Or do you have just one layer of healing?

Tim: Oh, I had to go back to that scene several times.

Question: Why?

Tim: God would show me more about the scene.

Question: What, about your mom? Her motive, her intent, her past?

Tim: Oh yeah. My mom saw her dad actually beat her mom. Fear gripped my mom early on. She didn't receive hugs either when she got older.

Question: So now that you know this about your mom's past, do you have compassion for her?

Tim: Yes. I know that she was wounded.

Question: Do you feel like you've overcome the emotion of rejection? Or are you still triggered sometimes?

Tim: Sometimes I feel that. I just go to Jesus and ask Him what He has to say about it.

Question: Do you feel a release each time?

Tim: Yes. I know now that if I'm triggered with a negative emotion, I can ask the Holy Spirit where that comes from and to take me to the scene. So I'll go back into the scene and ask Jesus what He has to say and He tells me.

1. Can you think back to a time in your life where you felt pain? Describe here.

   _____
   _____
   _____
   _____
   _____

2. Are you able to go back into that scene (in your mind) and look for Jesus? If yes, please describe what He is doing or saying.

   _____
   _____
   _____
   _____
   _____
   _____
   _____
   _____
   _____
   _____
   _____
   _____
   _____

3. Does His presence and words give you comfort?
   Yes/No/Some Comfort

   _____
   _____
   _____
   _____

4. Search the Scriptures to find promises from God that He will always be there for you and comfort you. Write them here and meditate on them. For an example from Tim's experience, see Appendix B "Dialogue With God While Reading Ephesians."

5. List a few "God-moments" when you were convinced that He was there, intervening in your life.

> *But this kind of demon does not go out except by prayer and fasting.*
> Matthew 17:21 (AMP)

5 FASTING

Fasting has been one of the most powerful ways to grow closer to God spiritually while healing the body simultaneously.

Occasions For Fasting

Throughout the Bible, fasting is mentioned for many of life's challenges, including preparing for battle, for healing, for repentance, for clarity and intimacy with God, and for a breakthrough.

Types Of Fasts

While there are many ways to fast, there are three types of fasts we want to briefly highlight from the Bible.

Daniel Fast: While in training to serve King Nebuchadnezzar, Daniel turned down royal food and wine and asked to eat only vegetables and drink water for ten days. At the end of the ten days, Daniel looked healthier and better nourished. In Daniel 1:17, it states that God gave them knowledge and understanding of all kinds of literature and learning. Daniel could understand dreams and visions, which became useful because he was the only one who could interpret King Nebuchadnezzar's dreams.

Esther Fast: In order to save the lives of the Jews in Susa, Esther abstained from both water and food for three days with her people. She was able to obtain favor with the king, who granted her request and had Haman, their enemy, hanged on the gallows that were originally prepared for Mordecai.

40 Day Fast: Jesus was led by the Spirit into the desert for forty days. He was tempted by the devil during this time and ate nothing. He successfully overcame the temptations and spoke the word of God (truth) into every manipulated scripture the enemy tried to use against him. When Jesus completed the forty day fast, he returned to Galilee in the power of the Spirit. (Luke 4).

Moses also went on a fast for forty days while recording the Ten Commandments. (Exodus 34:28)

In these 3 types of Biblical fasts, there is a self-discipline that takes place in order to hear from God clearly and complete Kingdom assignments.

What Happens To The Body During A Fast

STAGE 1: (Day 1-2)

Your body begins a process called gluconeogenesis, which is when the liver converts non-carbohydrate materials into glucose. Your heart rate and blood pressure will lower and your metabolism will become more efficient.

STAGE 2: (Day 3-7)

Your energy level will increase and you will have fewer hunger pains. In this stage, ketosis begins. This is when the body starts to burn stored fat and use it as a power source. This stage is ideal for weight loss and balancing blood sugar levels.

STAGE 3: (DAY 8-15)

Your mental clarity and mood will see dramatic improvements. Your body enters "healing mode" as it releases free radicals, toxins, and stressors. You will become stronger and your immune system more resilient.

STAGE 4: (Day 16 and Beyond)

If you fast this long, you need to be under the close supervision of a trusted healthcare professional. A steady balance will set in as your body continues to heal and cleanse itself.

STAGE 5: (Ending the Fast)

Ending your fast is just as important as beginning the practice. It is recommended to ease back into the digestive process with liquids like bone broth, smoothies, and juices. Avoid solid foods until your internal system acclimates - this time frame depends on how long you fasted.

For more information about fasting, we highly recommend *Fasting* by Jentzen Franklin.

Keisha Sowers - A Story Of Prophetic Gift Activated During An Extended Fast.

Q: Can you tell me about a significant fasting experience you've had?

Keisha: In my early 30s, I went on a spiritual journey and moved to Chicago for a while. It was more of a forced fast because I didn't have a steady job yet and didn't know what I was going to eat the next day. Or the day after that. So I had to live life by faith.

I remember being in the apartment, rent was due, and there was no food in the fridge. I was praying to God, worshipping Him, and focused on Him instead of the situation. I felt my spirit connect with His. The hunger pains went away - it was as if they lifted - and I felt more spiritual rather than physical. I felt as if I was above the circumstances. There was peace from just knowing that He was with me.

While fasting, there was one point when I felt the Holy Spirit rise up and say through my mouth, "Pour out more love on my people!" That had never happened to me before. I don't go around saying things like that. I thought, "Whoa, what is that", and then realized that God was speaking through me. That was the day the prophetic activated in my life.

Q: What did you gain from that experience?

Keisha: I was then able to hear from God more clearly and be a mouthpiece for Him. His peace took over the situation and it helped increase my faith. Miraculously, I was able to get out of that situation. It wasn't because of my own striving or performance. It was because of resting in Him, spending time loving on Him and believing that He was going to pull me through.

We recommend to those who come to us for a healing session to fast the day BEFORE and the day OF the session.

NEXT STEP:

1. Do you feel God is calling you to a fast during your inner healing process? If yes, what type of fast?
   _____
   _____

2. How long? _____

3. Write out your plan to stay the course.

_____
_____
_____
_____
_____
_____
_____
_____
_____
_____
_____
_____
_____
_____
_____
_____
_____
_____
_____
_____
_____
_____
_____
_____

Let the words of my mouth and the meditation of my heart be acceptable in Your sight, O LORD, my Rock and my Redeemer.
Psalm 104:34

6 TRUTH MEDITATION

I'm going to share about the way I viewed my dad.

I saw him and judged him of being angry, controlling, and heavy-handed.

He had "the look" too, that once you saw that, you knew to stop what you were doing. I ended up being the same way.

One time during a prayer session with some close friends, I asked them to help me through this. As I was sitting in the chair, I began to forgive my dad and began to break some judgments and vows I had made against him.

As I finished forgiving, I saw this vision of Jesus. He came and said, "Come with Me, I want to take you somewhere." So I went with Him and I was in heaven in front of this throne and the Father was sitting there with His hands on His lap.

I quickly turned my head, because I was taught that if you looked at God you would die. He began to speak to me and tell me that He didn't discipline like my earthly dad. Father God said He reasoned with me.

I began to feel more at ease and the next thing I knew I had crawled up on Father God's lap. He began to explain to me why my dad disciplined the way he did. His dad was shot and killed when he was 16 years old and he became an instant parent to 6 siblings. He learned he could get them to do what he wanted through anger and control. So he used that with myself and my brothers.

That's the way I saw it. My brothers may have seen it differently.

When God finished speaking, I got up from His lap and began to walk away.

Then I heard Father God say, "Tim, you know the way, come back as often as you like." Wow, I was so in awe of what Father God had just said to me. And I did that ... I would run back into the throne room and jump into His lap.

I still do that to this day.

Reflections from the experience:
One of the greatest lessons I learned from this was to stop judging others.

I use to follow up my judgments with a vow, that I won't be like that. We all have our own issues and we don't really know what others have been through in their lives. I've learned that hurt people, hurt people. That is, until they get their healing.

When I feel offended by someone, I take it to the Lord and see what He has to say about it. Most of the time, He has me pray for the person who has hurt me. He shows me the good intentions they have but they may not say it or give it in what I think is an edifying way. The truth is there, but not the tone or emotion they are delivering it in.

In John 8:32, Jesus says, "You shall know the truth and the truth shall set you free". That's true when you seek truth and not dwell in offense. Afterwards, He may show me something that I may need to work on within myself.

Now See This The Way God Sees It.

Challenge: Is there a person or circumstance in your life currently that has skewed your perspective to the negative? Ask God to show you the good in this ... then speak that goodness into the atmosphere and over the person.

Scripture Meditation:

Genesis 1:31
God saw all that He made, and it was very good.

Romans 8:28
And we know that in all things God works for the good of those who love Him, who have been called according to His purpose.

_____
_____
_____
_____
_____
_____
_____
_____
_____
_____
_____
_____
_____
_____
_____
_____
_____
_____
_____
_____

In Appendix D, use the Truth Meditation chart to support your journey of replacing lies and negative thoughts with truth. Write down what God has to say about you and the situation. Ask Him to show you supporting scripture to meditate on as well.

7 SOAKING

Resting in God's presence is one of the most important aspects of the day.

The difference between soaking and the new age version of meditation is that soaking focuses only on Yeshua. The mind is filled with interactions with Him and His Glory during that time.

Many people choose to "soak" in His Presence in the morning. Some prefer at night. You can set the length of time to rest, and schedule it daily (we recommend), weekly, or as needed.

When we start a session, we have people soak for about 10 minutes before we start.

There are different ways to soak.

1. **Soaking With Anointed Music.**

    We use a Spotify playlist filled with the Holy Spirit inspired music. You can create your own as you needed. Choose the pace of music you feel your spirit needs during your soaking time and let the music minister to your spirit and help usher in the peace of God.

    Music Pace

    While many times, we use soft music for soaking, there are times where fast-paced, celebratory music is need it. Your dance, praise, and worship lifting up to God is part of the experience and can activate joy, gratefulness, and conquer emotions like depression and anxiety.

2. **Soaking In The Blood Of Jesus And The Dunamis Power Of Jesus.**

    When healing soul wounds, Katie Souza recommends soaking in the blood of Yeshua to wash the wound clean and then receiving the Dunamis power of Jesus to cauterize the wound.

    For more information and resources about this type of soaking, visit KatieSouza.com

3. **Soaking In Scripture.**

   Another way to soak is to meditate on the audio version of scripture. If you need healing, play healing scriptures. If you need provision, play scriptures that focus on God providing for your needs like Matthew 6:25, 2 Corinthians 9:8, and Deuteronomy 28. YouTube has many videos like this so you can soak in scripture. Most of the videos are free.

In Appendix E, there are a few journal pages to record what God says and what you see during your soaking time.

Activate:

Do you currently soak? If yes, how can you improve your soaking time at this point in your spiritual journey? We also recommend adding the Cellular Cleansing Prayer located in Appendix A to your soaking time as needed.

APPENDIX

APPENDIX A

CELLULAR CLEANSING PRAYER

"Cellular Cleansing Prayer" © 2018. Used by permission and contributed by Vaterio Hunter. Voice of Many Waters International AACML

Cleansing on a cellular level is dealing with cellular memory.

Many times we find that the trauma that has taken place in the generational line and in someone's personal life, can cause a ripple effect in the cells. Because cells have cellular memory, they tend to remember the trauma, and relay the frequency of that trauma back into the body.

This is a prayer for the cleansing of the cells and cellular memory.

Heavenly Father,

I come to you asking you to cleanse me on the cellular level concerning _____. I confess that in the past I or my ancestors have committed the following sins that have caused an echo in my life on a cellular level _____. I renounce and repent from the sins of _____ on behalf of myself and my ancestors on both sides of my family, all the way back to Adam and Eve.

I also forgive my ancestors, and those who brought harm or offended my ancestors for the offenses of _____, that opened the door for a cellular echo in my bloodline. In specific I forgive _____. I also forgive myself for where I committed _____ against myself and my bloodline.

I now break every recompense that came upon my life and my bloodline down to the cellular level. I also break every curse spoken against my life and my bloodline from myself or others down to the cellular level. In particular I break the curses and recompenses as follows _____. In the name of Jesus.

I command my cells to be cleansed now, I command cleansing in the nucleus, in the cell membrane, in the cytoplasm, in the endoplasmic reticulum, in the ribosomes, in the golgi body, in the lysosomes, in the mitochondria, in the vacuoles, and in the cilia and flagella, in the name of Jesus.

I command my cells to return to the original design that God created for them to be. I command my cellular memory to be restored and to remember and reflect my identity in Christ. In the name of Jesus.

APPENDIX B
A DIALOGUE WITH GOD WHILE READING EPHESIANS

Eph. 1:

1. God's holy people who are faithful followers of Christ Jesus
   You are one of those Tim. (I wept at this)

2. May grace and peace be yours, sent to you from God our Father and Jesus Christ our Lord.
   Ask Me for grace and peace.

3. Father of our Lord Jesus Christ, who has blessed us with every spiritual blessing in the heavenly realms because we belong to Christ.
   You asked for these the other day Tim, and you saw these, don't stop asking. I gladly pour these out on you and those you ask Me to pour them out on. Keep asking.

4. God loved us and chose us in Christ to be holy and without fault in His eyes.
   You are forgiven and without fault. Forgive yourself and don't let the enemy beat you up with guilt.

5. His unchanging plan has always been to adopt us into His own family by bringing us to Himself through Jesus Christ. And this gave Him great pleasure.
   You do give me great pleasure Tim, (I wept again), accept it, you do and you bring others pleasure. (I continued to weep)

6. Wonderful kindness He has poured out on us because we belong to His dearly loved Son.

7. He is so rich in kindness that He purchased our freedom through the blood of His Son, and our sins are forgiven.
   You are free from sin and guilt and alive unto righteousness.

8. He has showered His kindness on us, along with all wisdom and understanding
   You have the mind of Christ, use it.

9. God's secret plan has now been revealed to us; it is a plan centered on Christ.

10. At the right time He will bring everything together under the authority of Christ - everything in heaven and on earth.

11. We have received an inheritance from God, for He chose us from the beginning, and all things happen just as He decided long ago.

12. Praise our glorious God.
    Praise Me Tim, even in the trials and sorrows. I am still in control.

13. God saves you, He identified you as His own by giving you the Holy Spirit.
    I will not let the Godly slip and fall, I uphold you with My victorious right hand. I'm not going to leave you.

14. The Spirit is God's guarantee that He will give us everything He promised and that He Has purchased us to be His own people. This is just one more reason for us to praise our glorious God.

15. Asking God, the glorious Father of our Lord Jesus Christ, to give you spiritual wisdom and understanding, so that you might grow in your knowledge of God.
    Keep asking and seeking, and watch what I do.

16. I pray that your hearts will be flooded with light so that you can understand the wonderful future He has promised to those He called. I want you to realize what a rich and glorious inheritance He has given to His people.
    Hang in there. You will see the work I'm doing in you and it will all come together for good.

17. I pray that you will begin to understand the incredible greatness of His power for us who believe Him. This is the same mighty power 20 that raised Christ from the dead and seated Him in the place of honor at God's right hand in the heavenly realms. 21 Now He is far above any ruler or authority or power or leader or anything else in this world or in the world to come. 22 And God has put all things under the authority of Christ, and He gave him this authority for the benefit of the church. 23 And the church is His body; it is filled by Christ, who fills everything everywhere with His presence.
    Remember " I AM!" And I AM for you.

APPENDIX C

HEART CHECK WORKSHEET

Date: _____

1. Heartwall?

2. Top 5 emotions

    1. _____ Mine/Generational

    2. _____ Mine/Generational

    3. _____ Mine/Generational

    4. _____ Mine/Generational

    5. _____ Mine/Generational

3. Ask God to talk to you about the scene where you first felt this emotion. Write down what He says.

_____
_____
_____
_____

4. Bring Jesus into the scene. What is He doing and/or saying?

_____
_____
_____
_____

5. Can we release the negative emotion now?

_____
_____
_____
_____

6. If not, write down what God is saying that you need to do in order to release the negative emotion.

_____
_____
_____

APPENDIX C

HEART CHECK WORKSHEET

Date: _____

1. Heartwall?

2. Top 5 emotions

   1.   Mine/Generational
   2.   Mine/Generational
   3.   Mine/Generational
   4.   Mine/Generational
   5.   Mine/Generational

3. Ask God to talk to you about the scene where you first felt this emotion. Write down what He says.

   _____
   _____
   _____
   _____

4. Bring Jesus into the scene. What is He doing and/or saying?

   _____
   _____
   _____
   _____

5. Can we release the negative emotion now?

   _____
   _____
   _____
   _____

6. If not, write down what God is saying that you need to do in order to release the negative emotion.

   _____
   _____
   _____

APPENDIX C

HEART CHECK WORKSHEET

Date: _____

1. Heartwall?

2. Top 5 emotions

   1. _____ Mine/Generational
   2. _____ Mine/Generational
   3. _____ Mine/Generational
   4. _____ Mine/Generational
   5. _____ Mine/Generational

3. Ask God to talk to you about the scene where you first felt this emotion. Write down what He says.
   _____
   _____
   _____
   _____

4. Bring Jesus into the scene. What is He doing and/or saying?
   _____
   _____
   _____
   _____

5. Can we release the negative emotion now?
   _____
   _____
   _____
   _____

6. If not, write down what God is saying that you need to do in order to release the negative emotion.
   _____
   _____
   _____
   _____

APPENDIX C
HEART CHECK WORKSHEET

Date: _____

1. Heartwall?

2. Top 5 emotions

    1.   Mine/Generational

    2.   Mine/Generational

    3.   Mine/Generational

    4.   Mine/Generational

    5.   Mine/Generational

3. Ask God to talk to you about the scene where you first felt this emotion. Write down what He says.

_____
_____
_____
_____

4. Bring Jesus into the scene. What is He doing and/or saying?

_____
_____
_____
_____

5. Can we release the negative emotion now?

_____
_____
_____
_____

6. If not, write down what God is saying that you need to do in order to release the negative emotion.

_____
_____
_____

APPENDIX C

HEART CHECK WORKSHEET

Date: _____

1. Heartwall?

2. Top 5 emotions

    1. _____ Mine/Generational
    2. _____ Mine/Generational
    3. _____ Mine/Generational
    4. _____ Mine/Generational
    5. _____ Mine/Generational

3. Ask God to talk to you about the scene where you first felt this emotion. Write down what He says.
   _____
   _____
   _____
   _____

4. Bring Jesus into the scene. What is He doing and/or saying?
   _____
   _____
   _____
   _____

5. Can we release the negative emotion now?
   _____
   _____
   _____
   _____

6. If not, write down what God is saying that you need to do in order to release the negative emotion.
   _____
   _____
   _____

APPENDIX D

TRUTH MEDITATION CHART

Lie	What God Says	Supporting Scripture
1		
2		
3		
4		
5		
6		
7		
8		

APPENDIX D

TRUTH MEDITATION CHART

Lie	What God Says	Supporting Scripture
1		
2		
3		
4		
5		
6		
7		
8		

APPENDIX D

TRUTH MEDITATION CHART

Lie	What God Says	Supporting Scripture
1		
2		
3		
4		
5		
6		
7		
8		

APPENDIX D

TRUTH MEDITATION CHART

Lie	What God Says	Supporting Scripture
1		
2		
3		
4		
5		
6		
7		
8		

APPENDIX D

TRUTH MEDITATION CHART

Lie	What God Says	Supporting Scripture
1		
2		
3		
4		
5		
6		
7		
8		

APPENDIX E
SOAKING JOURNAL

Date_____

APPENDIX E
SOAKING JOURNAL

Date_____

APPENDIX E
SOAKING JOURNAL

Date_____

APPENDIX E
SOAKING JOURNAL

Date_____

APPENDIX E
SOAKING JOURNAL

Date_____

BOOKS AND RESOURCES

Milan Yerkovich and Kay Yerkovich, How We Love (Colorado Springs: WaterBrook, Expanded edition, 2009), 418 pages

Keisha Sowers, Adventure: The 90 Day Spiritual Challenge (Christian Faith Publishing, Inc., 2018), 302 pages

Jentzen Franklin, Fasting (Florida: Charisma House, 2007), 258 pages

Art Mathias, In His Own Image: We Are Wonderfully Made (Dr. Art Marthias, 2010), 244 pages

Katie Souza, Healing The Wounded Soul (Florida: Charisma House, 2017), 224 pages

Dr. Caroline Leaf, Switch On Your Brain (Michigan: Baker Books; Reprint edition, 2015), 240 pages

ABOUT THE AUTHORS

Tim and Keisha Sowers are the founders of The Sowers Ministries.

They have written several books and host healing retreats and training in West Palm Beach, Florida USA to empower people in the inner healing process. They would love to hear from you and support you on your spiritual journey.

📷 @thesowersfamily

f TimandKeisha Sowers